The *Donoghue* Agency
Innovative Sales and Management Training / Consulting

Fred de Avila
President

Agents of Wilson Learning Corporation
18 Technology Drive, Suite 152, Irvine CA 92718 • (714) 753-1688

THE SITUATIONAL LEADER

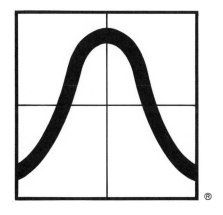

Dr. Paul Hersey

The Center for Leadership Studies

to Suzanne

The Situational Leader

is published by
The Center for Leadership Studies
230 W. Third Avenue
Escondido, CA 92025
(619) 741-6595

You may obtain additional copies of this book from the distributor:
University Associates
8517 Production Avenue
San Diego, CA 92121
(619) 578-5900

Library of Congress Catalog Number 84-072125
ISBN 0-931619-00-9

Foreword

This is an exciting period in understanding management practices and problems. There is an urgent awareness that the utilization of human resources is the real test of overall organizational success. The outcomes in our search for excellence will be the result of how we manage our people. It is *our people* that will determine whether we become one of the 100 best managed companies or whether we even survive as an organization.

University curricula focus on technical and conceptual skills and tend to pay only lip service to teaching the critically important skills of managing people. The situation is not a great deal better in the work place. Many managers have not had the benefit of effective training, and opportunities for mentoring are rare. We cannot count on observation and modeling as processes by which we can develop competent human resource managers. And much of the training that is offered tends to be either situation specific or superficial.

What has long been needed is a system for managing people that is both conceptual and practical. An easy to grasp system with a scope that is broad enough to permit its application to a wide range of situations is essential. Such a model would promote a precise language in which managers could both understand and act upon the problems they experience in managing their people. This new approach must build on the existing language of management so that learning it and using it are easily mastered. Furthermore, this model must have face validity that allows it to be accepted and implemented from the executive suite to the first level of supervision.

The Situational Leadership model, developed by Dr. Paul Hersey and his colleagues at the Center for Leadership Studies, meets these criteria. The vitality and acceptance of this approach is demonstrated by the large number of training programs that are now utilizing the model throughout the world.

For the first time, in a brief, succinct, and easy to read text, we can benefit from the application of the Situational Leadership model. *The Situational Leader* is a handy reference guide and dramatically illustrates the generality of its application. This slim volume provides a brief but powerful introduction to Situational Leadership.

I believe that this volume represents a significant contribution to our continuing search to improve the quality of managing our most precious resource—our people.

J. William Pfeiffer, Ph.D.,J.D.
President
University Associates, Inc.
San Diego, California

Table of Contents

Prologue

It was inevitable. Everybody knew it was coming. Taylor's department had been outperforming all the other departments for two solid years. Costs were down, turnover was almost non-existent, and chronic absenteeism was a thing of the past. More innovative ideas had come out of Taylor's department than from all the others combined. In addition, there was an observable sense of pride within the group. Without question, Taylor was the most qualified person in the company to take a step forward.

Top management was both elated and concerned. There was no question that Taylor would shine like a star in the new job. But replacing that kind of expertise would be tough. Naturally, the company supported Taylor's recommendation of Rogers as a replacement. Rogers looked very good on paper. The question was, could Rogers maintain the momentum and the productivity?

Introduction

This is the story of a Situational Leader. It's a story of a manager who is under the gun to achieve results, develop subordinates, and contribute to organizational success. This book is intended to help *you* maximize *your* potential as a leader and as a manager because sometimes things just don't turn out the way they're supposed to—*especially when other people are involved.*

It's a common problem. Normally, little can be accomplished without the cooperation of others. At home, in social settings, or on the job, you're often in situations where the behavior of other people determines your success.

Now that you've searched for excellence... analyzed the megatrends... and learned what a manager can do in one minute, it's time to consider *the other 59 Minutes.* What you need is a practical model to help identify strategies for meeting the ongoing challenges encountered in leadership situations. Leading and managing is a full time job that should be practiced *every hour of every day.*

Often leadership and management tools are not put to use by the practitioners for which they were designed. Somewhere between the "ivory tower" and the "shop floor" most theories lose their impact. It's tragic that so much useful information is discarded. The reason these theories have not been put to use is that the information has seldom been translated into *practical models* that can be replicated and applied.

It may be appropriate at this time to note the difference between a model and a theory. A theory attempts to explain or interpret *why* things happen as they do. Theories deal with insight. As such they are not designed to recreate events. A model, on the other hand, is a pattern of already existing events which can be learned and therefore repeated. For example, in trying to imagine *why* Henry Ford was motivated to mass produce automobiles you would be dealing with theory. However, if you recorded the procedures and sequences necessary for mass production of automobiles, this would be a model.

This book presents a particular model, the Situational Leadership model. The format of each of the seven chapters consists of three parts: The Story, The Background, and The Epilogue. "The Story" is an interaction between the boss and a newly appointed manager. "The Background" develops, explains, and applies Situational Leadership. "The Epilogue" summarizes key points and provides a transition into the next chapter.

Let's get on with the story......

CHAPTER ONE

Managing People

THE STORY

It's Monday morning. The first Monday morning in two years that Taylor has not been out on the shop floor. All eyes seem to be on Rogers. The General Manager, who Rogers now reports to, has stopped by to discuss Taylor's impressive track record and to make sure that the transition goes as smoothly as possible. After the cordial greetings and the customary cup of coffee, Rogers' boss poses the inevitable question . . . . .

General Manager: Well, I don't think I have to tell you that you're filling some pretty big shoes out there . . . how do you feel about it?

Rogers: I'd be lying if I told you I wasn't a little bit nervous but I honestly think I'm prepared. Taylor and I spent a lot of time discussing Leadership and Management.

General Mgr:	Leadership and Management! You mean there's a difference?
Rogers:	Yes. I think there's a distinct difference. Management to me is working with all the people here in the department to accomplish our weekly and quarterly goals. Leadership, as I see it, *is any time I attempt to get somebody else to do something for me.* That could be the people who are going to be working for me, my counterparts in the other departments, or even you.
General Mgr:	That's interesting. What are some of the other things you and Taylor talked about... maybe you can save us both some time.
Rogers:	Well, Taylor talked about the importance of measuring results in two ways.
General Mgr:	Two ways?
Rogers:	I know things have to be done in terms of company standards and specifications. But I also know the impact I'll have on the

people that work for me. It's not enough just to get results. I have to get people turned on about their work and keep them that way.

General Mgr: That's something that Taylor managed to do very well. How do you plan to tackle that one?

Rogers: As a start, I have to understand a little bit about what makes people tick.... You know, think through some of the reasons why people behave the way they do. If I can get a handle on that, the next step is to be able to predict how they will act when I assign them a job to accomplish, and then see if I can get them to focus on what's best for the department and the company.

General Mgr: Oh...a little manipulation, huh?

Rogers: Well, I guess you could call it that...but manipulation to me is one of those terms that has more than one meaning.

General Mgr: So how do *you* define it?

Rogers: Let's just say this, I don't plan to use deceit or influence over others for my own personal gain. But, I do have every intention of focusing everyone's efforts in a direction that will benefit each individual and the department.

General Mgr: I'd be pretty hard pressed to argue with that one.

THE BACKGROUND

The key to being an effective manager is *leadership*.

Some concepts in the behavioral sciences are well intended, but fall short of the mark. They give you some good ideas to think about, but they don't always tell you *how* or *when* to put these ideas into practice. Woody Allen says that success in life is "...20% timing and 80% just showing up." People usually "show up" in leadership situations. But leadership success is much more than just showing up. It is the application of tested concepts and the "timing" skills necessary to get things done. This book is designed to provide you with these skills.

Influencing the behavior of others should not be thought of as a single event. It's a full-time job in which every minute must be spent wisely. The strategy presented will help you maximize results when working with people. Sometimes this is easier said than done. Real-life situations are never static. They're in a constant state of change. Things are either getting better or getting worse.

If you're looking for a single formula to apply in every situation, let's agree that there's no magic solution for leaders. Like any other skill, leadership effectiveness increases the more you understand and practice the skills.

Begin at the Beginning

In Lewis Carroll's classic story of Alice In Wonderland, the Red Queen tells Alice to " . . . begin at the beginning and end at the end." That's also good advice for approaching the subject of managing people.

Let's begin by defining *leadership:*

> Leadership is any attempt to influence the behavior of another individual or group.

Leadership refers to situations in which you're working with others. This book is *not* about doing things yourself. It's about accomplishing tasks and reaching goals through the efforts of other people. Effective leaders *make* things happen. They don't sit around watching other people and waiting to react to whatever situations occur. They know what ought to happen, plan a way to make it happen, and take steps to see that it does!

Contrast leadership with management:

> Management is working with and through others to accomplish organizational goals.

This applies to more than just business. It applies to any organization. . . . family, community, Little League, church, or garden club. Whatever the setting, managing is working with others to accomplish *organizational goals*.

Leadership is a much broader concept than management. You can have a variety of different objectives in mind when you attempt to influence other people. In reality, management is a special form of leadership that involves the goals of an organization. Leadership itself can be attempted for any reason.

In leadership situations, our outcomes vary. Let's consider an example:

> It's Wednesday afternoon. After asking an employee to finish the weekly report, you leave for a late meeting. Without specific instructions, the person misses quite a number of details in hurrying through the report. At quitting time the papers are dropped on your desk and the employee heads for the parking lot. The next morning you inspect the report and find several major entries missing. You shrug and redo the job yourself.
>
> The next day the same employee is having a tough time meeting a project deadline. By persuading co-workers to lend a hand and monitoring their progress, the employee gets the job finished on time.

In both cases the job gets done. But let's look at these examples in terms of *leadership.* In the first, your attempt at leadership was unsuccessful. You ended up doing the work. In the second example, the project was completed through the efforts of others, and therefore the attempt at leadership was successful with the co-workers. The employee was successful in influencing the behavior of others in that particular situation. But the attitudes of the same people toward working with that person in the future need to be considered.

Suppose that the employee neglects to thank the co-workers and to share the praise for the job well done. They might be upset at the way they were treated and probably wouldn't help in the future. In this case, although the project was completed once, that person would be hard pressed to get help next time.

Some leaders can be successful in the short term but ineffective in the long term. In evaluating leadership attempts, consideration needs to be given to the impact on the people being influenced. Leaders need to get a job done, but they also need to build continuing cooperation. The illustration on the opposite page shows the two outcomes of attempted leadership. Success has to do with how well the job gets done and effectiveness has to do with people's attitude about performing the work.

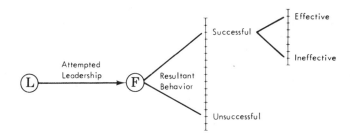

Illustration 1

In management, the difference between successful and effective leadership attempts often explains why many supervisors can get results when they are right there looking over the worker's shoulder. But as soon as they leave, output declines and often such things as horseplay and scrap loss increase.

To bridge the gap between one-time success and long-term effectiveness, you need to develop three skills in working with people. These skills are essential whether you're a manager on the job, a parent in the home, or a teacher in the classroom.

1. *Understanding* people's past behavior.
   Recognize why people did what they did... what motivated them...what evoked the behavior that helped or hindered the accomplishment of tasks.
2. *Predicting* future behavior.
   Understanding why people behaved in a certain way is not enough. You also need to be able to predict how they will behave in the future under the same conditions but in the rapidly changing environment of today's world.
3. *Directing, changing* and *controlling* behavior.
   Understanding past behavior and predicting future behavior are still not enough. You must also accept the responsibility for *influencing* the behavior of others in accomplishing tasks and reaching goals.

These are the three skills that determine whether leadership attempts will be successful or unsuccessful, effective or ineffective. Understanding what motivates people, predicting how they will behave in response to your leadership attempts, and directing their behavior, are all necessary for effective leadership.

Note that the first two skills are passive in nature. Understanding and predicting do not require actions involving other people. The key to obtaining results is directing, changing and controlling the efforts of people in the accomplishment of organizational goals. That's where the leader translates thoughts and intentions into end results.

Controlling People

People who hear the word *control* often ask, "Does that mean we have to manipulate others?" Words that suggest control and manipulation sometimes have a negative meaning to many people. However, when you accept the role of leader, you also accept the responsibility for channeling the behavior of others toward achieving results. That's true whether you're at work striving to gain the commitment of your people, or at home attempting to assist your children in developing their basic values.

It's also important to remember that words are simply packages of ideas and, as such, are often misinterpreted. If manipulation means taking unfair advantage, being deceitful, and influencing others for self interest, then it has a negative connotation. On the other hand, if manipulation means using influence strategies skillfully and managing people fairly for mutually rewarding and productive purposes, it's an appropriate and necessary means for goal accomplishment.

If you're still concerned about words like control or manipulation, think of it as training or facilitating. Whatever words are chosen, overall effectiveness depends upon *understanding, predicting,* and *influencing* the behavior of other people.

A Hammer Won't Always Do the Job

For every job there is an appropriate tool. Hammers are great for pounding nails. You could also use a hammer to cut a two by four but it would leave a lot of rough edges. For that particular activity there is probably a better tool. To build effectively you need a variety of tools and the knowledge of what they are designed to accomplish.

The same is true for leadership and management. It is unrealistic to think that a single tool is all that's needed to manage effectively. A trap many people fall into is the reliance on the latest fad to solve all their management problems. There seems to develop an unrealistic assumption of what this will do for them. Many useful management tools have been developed over the years. But the leader should know what to expect from them, and just as importantly, what not to expect.

You need to understand and be able to use different tools when leading and managing people. The concepts presented in the remaining chapters are intended to add to your "tool box" and increase your effectiveness as a leader.

THE EPILOGUE

Rogers:	I guess what I'm trying to say is, I know I have a big job here. I understand the importance of maintaining productivity and keeping people involved in their work. I think the biggest thing I have to do is be able to adapt my style to the different situations I will face.
General Mgr:	You mentioned style . . . exactly what do you mean by that?

CHAPTER TWO

Leadership Styles

THE STORY

Rogers:	Simply put, I guess my style would be the way other people see me behaving.
General Mgr:	Other people?
Rogers:	Right, it's how they interpret what I do that will influence them. Not so much how I see myself.
General Mgr:	Well, how do you see yourself, autocratic or democratic?
Rogers:	I really don't see myself as being autocratic or democratic because that's kind of an either/or description. I know there are times when I'll have to be directive with people telling them what to do, when to do, and how to do things. I also realize there are other times when it's appropriate to par-

	ticipate and involve others in the decision making. . . . more or less let them run with the ball.
General Mgr:	Well, are you more concerned about getting the job done or about your people? It's kind of hard to tell from your last statement.
Rogers:	I honestly believe you have to have a positive attitude about both. Sure I'm concerned about people, and I'm also concerned about the job. . . . I really think those are values you have to have to be a good manager.
General Mgr:	So with all that in mind, how do *you* treat your people?
Rogers:	To be honest, I haven't found *one* best way.

THE BACKGROUND

A leader's style can be described in various ways. Some managers can be called "tough and hard-nosed" while others might be termed "easy and permissive." Some managers could be considered "coaches" while others might be seen as "persuasive." There are many adjectives used to characterize the actions and statements of leaders when they are attempting to influence the behavior of others.

Let's define leadership style:

> The patterns of behavior (words and actions) of the leader *as perceived by others.*

Leadership style is defined in terms of how the leader appears *in the eyes of the beholder.* It's not how people see themselves that matters, but how they come across to others they're attempting to influence. You may see yourself as a very humanistic and caring person, but if your followers see you as hard-nosed and bossy, *their* perceptions, not *yours,* will affect their behavior.

Autocratic versus democratic leader styles

To explain more about leadership, early management theorists set up a scale which depicted two extreme leadership styles. Illustration 2 on the opposite page represents the autocratic/democratic scale.

Democratic   Autocratic

⬅━━━━━━━━━━━━━━━━━━━━━━━━━━━━━━━━━➡

Illustration 2

On one extreme, leadership styles were described as autocratic . . . on the other extreme, democratic. It was felt that any leader's style would fall between these two extremes.

Autocratic behavior was described as being directive. How do American history books remember General George Patton? To most observers he appeared to be an autocratic leader. He told his subordinates exactly what he wanted them to do, and rarely explained his decisions or asked for opinions. On the African desert or in the forests of Europe, everyone knew that Patton was the decision maker!

On the other hand, democratic leaders usually behaved in ways that helped their followers share information, make decisions and solve problems. King Arthur could be viewed as a democratic leader. He gave his knights plenty of opportunity to participate in discussions. Even the shape of his round table helped every member to contribute.

As managers were observed and their behavior recorded, it became clear that the autocratic and democratic labels did not describe accurately how they did things. As a result, the behaviors managers engaged in were classified as task behavior and relationship behavior.

Task Behavior

Task behavior is defined as:

> the extent to which the leader engages in
> spelling out the duties and responsibilities
> of an individual or group. The behaviors
> include telling people what to do, how to
> do it, when to do it, where to do it and
> who's to do it.

An example of high amounts of task behavior
might be the last time you went for a blood test. The
lab technician was probably very directive about it.
Ignoring your squirming, you were told to roll up
your sleeve and extend your arm. You were shown
how to squeeze your hand during the sampling and
when to do it. After the test was completed, you
received specific instructions about holding the cot-
ton swab over the area. You might have passed out
in the process, but the technician was going to get
the job done!

Notice that being directive doesn't mean being
nasty or short-tempered. The technician might have
been very friendly toward you, but the actions and
statements were aimed at completing the task. Task
behavior is characterized by one-way communication from the leader to the follower. The technician
was not interested in how you thought the blood
test should be performed.

Relationship Behavior

Relationship behavior is defined as:

> the extent to which the leader engages in two-way or multi-way communication if there is more than one person. The behaviors include listening, encouraging, facilitating, providing clarification, and giving socioemotional support.

Consider the organization that hires proven performers from one of their competitors. When these new employees report to work, it is important to encourage them to become a part of the team. In short, newcomers need to receive support from the boss. This is an example of high relationship behavior. The listening, encouraging, and facilitating a leader engages in characterize the two way communication which is distinctive of relationship behavior.

Attitude and Behavior

In looking at leadership style the focus is on behavior. There is a distinct difference between behavior and attitude. Behavior is what leaders say and do. An attitude is a feeling, value, or concern for or against something. It is a person's *behavior* that will evoke a response in *someone else.*

It is difficult to predict a behavior from an attitude. People who have similar attitudes or value sets about something may engage in a variety of different behaviors. For example, people who have a high concern for the problems in urban areas can act in different ways. Some avoid the issues altogether. Others provide sympathy and encouragement. Still others get actively involved and provide direction and guidance in an attempt to make changes. The same high concern evoked different behaviors. It is the *behavior* of people that impacts others, not their attitudes.

It is important for leaders, whether they be managers, leaders, or parents, to have a high concern for both end results and people. In order to capitalize on this high concern, a variety of leadership styles are needed to adapt to the different situations or problems a leader faces.

Leadership Styles

Managers observed in work settings used both task behavior and relationship behavior to influence their people. These two influence behaviors are separate and distinct dimensions. Managers were found successful using mainly high amounts of task behavior while others were successful using mainly high amounts of relationship behavior. Still other managers were successful using high amounts of both task behavior and relationship behavior. And there were managers who were successful using low amounts of both task behavior and relationship behavior. As such, a single continuum like the autocratic/democratic continuum, did not portray different leader behaviors accurately.

A more usable framework was necessary. First, task behavior and relationship behavior were placed in separate dimensions of a two dimensional graph. Second, four quadrants were constructed on the graph to identify the four basic leadership styles. The diagram on the opposite page illustrates these styles.

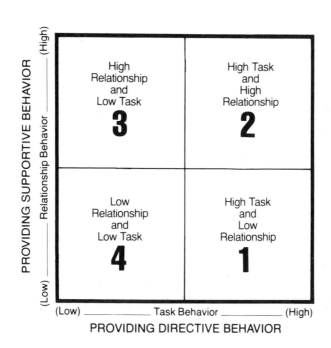

Illustration 3

Task behavior is plotted from low to high on the horizontal axis. Relationship behavior is plotted from low to high on the vertical axis. This makes it possible to describe leader behavior in four ways.

The following examples demonstrate different situations in which these styles can be used.

Style 1: (S1)

This leadership style is characterized by above average amounts of task behavior and below average amounts of relationship behavior.

Used Effectively:
A fire chief takes control during a four-alarm blaze. There's very little time to develop two-way communications, explain decisions, and ask the firefighters if they have any questions. To accomplish the task of putting out the fire and saving lives, the chief is very directive. Orders are issued without explanation and followers are watched closely to see that instructions are carried out to the letter.

Used Ineffectively:
The accounting department is going to move to new offices. The people in this department have been through the process before and have performed well. However, the manager sits them down, and gives them detailed instructions about who closes the files, boxes the records, and how to refile.

Leader Style 1 is directive. It consists of telling the individual or group what to do, when, where, how and with whom to do it. Style 1 is typified by one-way communication in which the leader directs the followers toward accomplishing tasks and reaching goals.

Style 2: (S2)

This leadership style is characterized by above average amounts of both task and relationship behavior.

Used Effectively:
An employee is promoted to a new job, and is eager to get started although unsure of how to go about it. The manager explains what's to be done and why each step is important. Before the meeting is over, the employee has time to ask questions and get clarification.

Used Ineffectively:
A supervisor's people are all "top hands" with plenty of experience. In department meetings the supervisor makes the decisions, and gives explanations about why certain procedures are required, even though the employees know as much as the supervisor about the tasks.

Leader Style 2 still provides guidance. The leader's actions and statements exhibit moderate to high amounts of task behavior. At the same time, the leader provides explanations and opportunities for clarification.

Style 3: (S3)

This leadership style is characterized by above average amounts of relationship behavior and below average amounts of task behavior.

Used Effectively:
> A new salesperson is about to make their first customer call on their own, but is still unsure of their abilities. Having confidence the salesperson can do it, the manager provides high amounts of support and encouragement and an opportunity to discuss things after the call.

Used Ineffectively:
> A work group asks their supervisor for direction on a newly assigned project. The supervisor responds by getting the group together and asking for suggestions, even though they have no knowledge or experience with this project.

Style 3 is characterized by leader behavior that provides encouragement, promotes discussion, and asks for contributions from the followers. This represents a big difference from Styles 1 and 2, where the leader provides the directions and makes the decisions.

Style 4: (S4)

This leadership style is characterized by below average amounts of both task behavior and relationship behavior.

Used Effectively:
> Your boss knows that you know how to prepare the monthly report, and that you have completed it on time in the past. In this case your boss lets you do your job with little input or direction.

Used Ineffectively:
> A new employee is having difficulty answering telephone inquiries from customers. The boss is asked how to handle certain questions but doesn't take time to help. As a result, not only is the employee frustrated but so are the customers.

Style 4 leader behavior provides little direction, and low amounts of two-way communication and supportive behavior.

THE EPILOGUE

Rogers: I guess the bottom line is that there are a variety of different leadership styles I could use. That's why I'm going to have to start looking at the people in this department differently than I did as a co-worker.

General Mgr: Why do you say that?

CHAPTER THREE

Assessing the Situation

THE STORY

Rogers: Although there are many things that come into play in getting the job done, Taylor used to say that if the follower decides not to follow, it's all over.

General Mgr: That sounds pretty simple.

Rogers: It's not that a lot of other things aren't important, or that managing is easy. It's just that the key to influencing others is to understand how committed and competent they are for the job you are asking them to do.

General Mgr: Well, you should have a pretty good handle on that. You've been around these people for quite a while.

Rogers: I know generally how they do their job, but that's not enough.

General Mgr: Why not?

Rogers: Well, Taylor explained it to me this way, and it really made sense. People *like* some jobs better than others, and people *do* some jobs better than others. That's why a general approach won't work. I have to look specifically at each person and what in particular I'm asking each of them to do.

THE BACKGROUND

Research has shown that a leader's success is affected by the environment. Because researchers wanted to know more about this environment and the factors that could determine the leader's effectiveness, they studied managers at work. The major factors they identified can affect the impact of *your* leadership style.

Leader effectiveness depends upon the interaction among the leader, follower, boss, associates, organization, job demands, and time constraints. These are the factors that tend to be present in the environment at any particular time. A change in one may create a change in the others. For instance, a back burner project that all of a sudden becomes priority "one" can cause change in a number of other factors.

The first factor is the *leader.* Leaders bring their leadership style to the situation. This is their pattern of behavior as perceived by others. Leaders also bring their attitudes to the situation. The leader is an important factor in the environment, but not the only one.

Followers also bring attitudes and behaviors to the situation, both individually and collectively. As such, followers develop distinct personalities. It isn't the patterns of behavior and values of the leader that determine effectiveness. It isn't the patterns of behavior and values of the followers, individually or as a group, that determine effectiveness. Effectiveness is determined by the interaction between the patterns of behavior and values of both the leader and the follower.

The leader's *boss* can also affect success. Everybody in an organization is accountable to someone. Even the president of a corporation has a boss, the chairman of the board. The chairman of the board reports to the stockholders. Most leaders are influenced by their boss.

Another variable is the key *associates* of the leader. Key associates are organizational peers whose cooperation is needed for the leader to get the job done.

Organizations also develop patterns of behavior and values that become characteristic and differentiate them from other organizations. It's not only the people who presently occupy top positions in organizations that impact corporate culture, it's also history and tradition.

Job demands are another variable. These are the followers' perceptions of the work the leader has them doing. If the followers are not interested in their work and would prefer not to be doing it, it may be necessary to use close supervision. However, if people are doing jobs that are exciting to them and that they find challenging, close supervision may not be required.

Another factor is the *time* available for making and implementing decisions. If a room catches on fire, it would be inappropriate for small groups to be formed to think through strategies for leaving. It would be appropriate for the leader to direct everyone out the safest door. The shorter the decision time, the more the leader is forced into using a more directive style.

There may be a number of other factors in the leader's situation. In attempting to influence the behavior of others, it's important to be aware of what's happening in the environment. Leaders sometimes find themselves "short-stopped" by one or more of the factors that exist.

Leaders cannot consistently be on top of all the variables within the environment on a moment to moment basis. The amount of data could be overwhelming. Research has shown that there is one variable that is crucial. This is the *relationship between the leader and follower.* If the follower decides not to follow, the other variables become unimportant. It is important, therefore, that leaders maximize their ability to manage the relationship with followers. A critical factor in determining success within the leader/follower relationship is the ability of the leader to correctly assess follower readiness.

Follower Readiness

Readiness is defined as the extent to which a follower has the ability and willingness to accomplish a specific task. Readiness levels vary. People tend to be at different levels of readiness depending on the task they are being asked to do. It is important to remember that readiness is not a personal characteristic. It is not an evaluation of a person's traits, values, age, etc. *Readiness is how a person performs at a particular task.*

Even though readiness depends on the task, it is sometimes necessary to break a job into the specific activities involved. For example, an engineer working on a project may be excellent at creative designing but far less competent for technical report writing. The more a leader can break down the activities of each job the more accurate the assessment of follower readiness.

The two major components of readiness are ability and willingness.

— *Ability* is the knowledge, experience and skill that an individual or group brings to a particular task or activity.

— *Willingness* has to do with confidence, commitment, and motivation to accomplish a specific task or activity.

Important to each of these definitions is the word "demonstrate." You need to judge readiness in terms of the behavior you see. Without demonstrated ability, you're only dealing with potential. Without demonstrated willingness, you're only dealing with "lip service," or simply intent without action.

Even though ability and willingness are different from each other they form an interacting influence system. One directly affects the other. The extent to which individuals have confidence, commitment and motivation affects the use of their present ability. It can also affect the degree to which they will grow and expand their present ability. Conversely, the amount of knowledge, experience and skill people bring to the job impacts their willingness. A significant change in one affects the whole.

An easy way to remember these components of readiness is to go back to the phrase used by children.... "ready, willing and able." Readiness is a person's willingness and ability to perform a specific job or function.

Readiness Levels

Readiness levels are the different combinations of ability and willingness that people bring to each task. The amounts of ability and willingness, from very high to very low, form four benchmark levels of readiness.

Readiness Level 1 (R1):

Unable and unwilling

The follower is unable and lacks commitment and motivation.

* An employee needs to learn how to operate new machinery. The employee does not know how to use the new machine, and has no interest or desire to learn.

Unable and insecure

The follower is unable and lacks confidence.

* A person takes their first flying lesson. The student has no idea what to do in the cockpit, and has no confidence in their ability to control the airplane.

Readiness Level 2 (R2):

Unable but willing
> The follower lacks ability but is motivated and making an effort.

> * The employee still lacks proficiency on the machine, but is making an effort to become qualified.

Unable but confident
> The follower lacks ability but is confident as long as the leader provides the guidance.

> * After a few lessons, the student pilot is still not able to fly the plane alone, but is enthusiastic and starting to feel confident as long as the instructor is still in the cockpit.

Readiness Level 3 (R3):

Able but unwilling

> The follower has the ability to perform the task but is not willing to use that ability.

> * The employee is already qualified on the machine but is now bored with the job.

Able but insecure

> The follower has the ability to perform the task, but is insecure or apprehensive about doing it alone.

> * Before the first solo flight, although the student has been qualified by the instructor, there is still some nervousness and apprehension about going it alone.

Readiness Level 4 (R4):

> Able and willing
>> The follower has the ability to perform and likes doing the job.
>
>> * The employee is qualified on the machine and enjoys operating it.

> Able and confident
>> The follower has the ability to perform and is confident about doing it alone.
>
>> * With a hundred hours of solo flight in the log book, the pilot is capable of flying the plane and very confident.

The importance of identifying these four readiness levels can be critical to effective leadership. Readiness levels can help leaders make decisions about what leadership styles will be most appropriate.

THE EPILOGUE

Rogers:

I think the whole idea here is that leadership is more than different strokes for different folks . . . . . it's different strokes for the same folks depending on what they happen to be doing and how they are performing. The key for me is to recognize those differences and change my style accordingly.

General Mgr:

Changing styles makes sense, but how do you figure out which styles will work for you?

CHAPTER FOUR

Selecting Appropriate Styles

THE STORY

Rogers:	Let me give you an example. When I first started working here, I found that one of my responsibilities was to plan and prepare a quarterly budget. The first time I tackled it, I didn't know where to start. Taylor broke out the budgetary manuals, gave me examples, told me what to consider, and how to itemize all the line items. In addition, I found that Taylor was never very far away in case I ran into a problem. I also remember that Taylor didn't ask me for a lot of input or suggestions. And looking back on it, that really made sense because being new and inexperienced, I really didn't have much to offer.
General Mgr:	Makes sense to me.

Rogers:
On the other hand, another job I had was to program the computer for the department's work schedules. I had been doing much the same thing for another company for three years before I came to work here. After a brief conversation with Taylor on specific scheduling requirements, Taylor turned me loose on the computer and asked me for any suggestions I might have for improvements.

General Mgr:
This is beginning to sound familiar. Going back to what you said earlier, it looks like Taylor took into consideration your competency and commitment, and acted accordingly.

Rogers:
You got it . . . . . and, you know, after a while, I could predict that Taylor would treat me differently depending on the job we had to do, how much I knew about it, and how much I wanted to get it done.

General Mgr:
So Taylor was actually consistent by being flexible?

Rogers: Exactly . . . and because of that I could ask for more guidance or more support whenever I needed it. I can remember times when I knew I was performing well but I just wanted Taylor to let me know things were on track. Then again there were times when I felt ready to be turned loose on a project and do it on my own.

General Mgr: Sounds like after a while you had as much to do with this process as Taylor did.

Rogers: No question about it. It became my responsibility to let Taylor know what I needed. We didn't always agree . . . but I never felt uncomfortable in asking.

General Mgr: Isn't there an awful lot involved here?

Rogers: I hope I haven't made this sound too complicated. Actually, you only have to ask yourself two questions. Is the person able to do the job? And is the person willing to do the job? I've found from past experience, if I

	start to lead before I've answered those two questions, I can run into some problems.
General Mgr:	What kind of problems?
Rogers:	When people don't know what to do, it's frustrating when they don't get the direction they need. And if people with experience and insight aren't given opportunities to share their ideas and take some responsibility, that can be frustrating too.

THE BACKGROUND

The importance of a leader's diagnostic ability cannot be over emphasized. As the ability and willingness of followers vary, leaders need to have the sensitivity and diagnostic ability to recognize and appreciate the differences. Yet even with good diagnostic skills, leaders may still be ineffective unless they can adapt their leadership style to meet the demands of their environment.

The foundation for the work involved in every profession is a learned repeatable process. Doctors make diagnostic judgements prior to prescribing treatment. As the symptoms and conditions change, the treatment may need to change. Theirs is not a trial and error or hit or miss endeavor; it is a rational process. Leaders and managers need a similar framework that provides them with a foundation for the leadership process.

It's not enough to know that there are four different leadership styles from which to choose. You need to consider each unique situation in order to understand which of the styles is most appropriate. In this chapter the Situational Leadership model is introduced. It provides a framework from which to diagnose different situations and prescribes which leader behaviors will have the highest probability of success.

Situational Leadership is based on an interplay among (1) the amount of task behavior a leader provides; (2) the amount of relationship behavior a leader provides; and (3) the readiness level that followers demonstrate in performing a specific task or activity. This model was developed to help you be more effective in your leadership attempts. It provides an understanding of the relationship between effective leadership styles and the readiness level of followers. Ability and willingness determine the readiness of an individual or group. Leadership style needs to match the readiness level of the followers.

For example, a professor who has a high readiness level for teaching is usually successful in classroom situations. At the same time, with paperwork, the professor's readiness level may be extremely low. The dean's request for reports and information ends up in a file marked, "Next year, if I'm not busy." These different readiness levels therefore affect the job of how the dean supervises. For the task of teaching students, the dean doesn't need to get involved at all. The professor is allowed to run with the ball. However, to get the reports completed, the dean's best course of action is quite different. The dean has to walk into the teacher's office and say, "I need this report right now, and here's how I want you to do it."

Effective leaders know how to "tailor" their styles to specific situations when attempting to influence the behavior of others. Why? Because in most situations, with individuals or groups, there is no all-purpose leadership style. The "missing link" in most approaches to leader effectiveness is the lack of a practical way to match leadership style to the needs of the follower. When attempting to influence others, your job is to (1) diagnose the readiness level of the follower for a specific task; and (2) provide the appropriate leadership style for that situation.

The Situational Leadership Model

The Situational Leadership model relates the four different levels of readiness to the four basic leadership styles. This provides the opportunity not only to assess follower behavior, but also to select high probability leadership styles. The following examples illustrate the Situational Leadership model.

Suppose as a leader you are given the task of influencing followers that are at opposite extremes in terms of their readiness to complete a task. Some have *all* the necessary knowledge, skill, confidence, and commitment, R4. The others have *no* knowledge, skill, confidence, or commitment, R1.

First consider the R1. If you have followers that are *completely unready*, how much guidance and direction are you going to have to provide? In this case you may have to provide *all* of it, telling them exactly what, where, when, and how to perform. How much supportive behavior should be provided? If people are not performing, and they are given significant amounts of strokes and support, you may be perceived as rewarding the lack of performance. You also have to be cautious how much two-way communication and supportive behavior is provided. This does not mean relationship behavior is non-existent. The leader needs a certain amount of two-way communication with followers to insure instructions are clear and they understand. In this case the high probability leadership style is high amounts of task and low amounts of relationship behavior, S1.

Now consider the R4. If you have followers that are *completely ready* to perform a task, how much guidance and direction are needed? You may not need to provide any instructions. In fact, there are cases where followers may have more expertise about a specific job than the leader. How much supportive behavior do you provide? These followers don't need a lot of head patting and supportive behavior. Give them the ball and let them run with it. This does not mean that relationship behavior is non-existent. The leader needs to touch base periodically to make sure the followers stay on track. And followers need a certain amount of feedback to let them know their contribution is noticed and appreciated. The high probability leadership style here is low amounts of task behavior and low amounts of relationship behavior, S4.

For different tasks and functions, most people are somewhere in between the extremes on the readiness scale. The unable but willing followers, R2, don't have the necessary knowledge or skill but are committed and eager to learn. Because they are still somewhat unable, they need guidance and direction. But since they're making an effort and trying, the leader needs to be supportive of that motivation. The high probability leadership style for these followers is high amounts of task behavior and high amounts of relationship behavior, S2.

The followers who have the necessary knowledge and skill to perform a specific task but lack confidence or motivation are R3's. The high probability leadership style for these followers is high amounts of relationship behavior but low amounts of task behavior, S3. They don't need a great deal of structure or direction because they have already demonstrated they know how to perform. But they need support. They need encouragement from the boss in order to build their confidence or dialogue and discussion to work through problems.

The Situational Leadership model is illustrated on the opposite page. The curved line through the four leadership styles represents the high probability combination of task behavior and relationship behavior. These combinations correspond to the readiness levels directly below. To use the model, select a point on the readiness continuum that represents follower readiness to perform a specific task. Then construct a perpendicular line from that point to a point where it intersects with the curved line representing leader behavior. This point indicates the most appropriate amount of task behavior and relationship behavior for that specific situation.

(HIGH)   **LEADER BEHAVIOR**

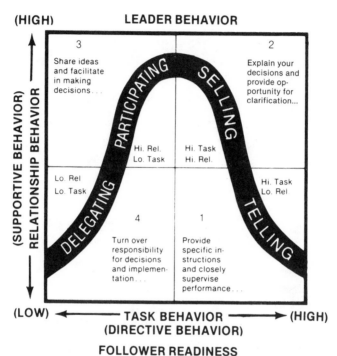

FOLLOWER READINESS

HIGH	MODERATE		LOW
R4	R3	R2	R1
Able & Willing or Motivated	Able but Unwilling or Insecure	Unable but Willing or Motivated	Unable & Unwilling or Insecure

Illustration 4

Notice the one-word descriptors for each of the four styles.

S1 is appropriate when attempting to influence low levels of readiness. It is called "Telling" because the leader provides the what, when, where and how. But the leader needs to be careful not to provide too much supportive behavior or it may be interpreted as permissive, easy, or rewarding a lack of performance.

S2 is appropriate when attempting to influence low to moderate levels of readiness. It is called "Selling" because the leader is still providing the direction and guidance. Through explaining why and clarification the leader attempts to get the follower to *buy into it* psychologically.

S3 is appropriate when attempting to influence moderate to high levels of readiness. It is called "Participating" because both leader and follower share in providing the guidance and direction. The leader's major role is facilitating and encouraging input and involvement from the followers.

S4 is appropriate when attempting to influence high levels of readiness. It is called "Delegating" because the leader turns over the responsibility for decision making and implementation to the follower.

These one-word descriptors are provided to make it easier to remember the four leadership styles. However, you may feel uncomfortable with one or more of these words in some situations. Words like telling, selling, participating and delegating may not always describe exactly what you intend to do. Here are some alternate words to help in describing these leader behaviors.

S1	S2	S3	S4
Telling	Selling	Participating	Delegating
Guiding	Explaining	Encouraging	Observing
Directing	Clarifying	Collaborating	Monitoring
Establishing	Persuading	Committing	Fulfilling

Using the Model

An understanding of follower needs is important. As people grow in their task-specific readiness, the behaviors they need from the leader also change. Followers who are performing at readiness levels 1 and 2 need structure and guidance in order to perform well and grow. They also need increased supportive behavior as they move from R1 to R2 as reward and reinforcement for their efforts.

Often managers will observe followers moving from being unable and insecure, R1, to unable but confident, R2. They perform well as long as the leader is there providing direction. It is important to note that the confidence and performance of R2 followers comes from the direction and feedback of the leader. It does *not* mean that they are able and confident to perform the task on their own.

The illustration on the opposite page helps to understand how insecurity will tend to increase again as the follower moves from R2 to R3. As people grow and are given the responsibility to accomplish tasks on their own, there is usually some apprehension with taking charge the first few times. Think about the first time you had to make a presentation in front of a group. Even though you practiced in front of a mirror and on a tape recorder, you probably had some "butterflies" and insecurity right before the moment of truth. But after you got a few "wins" under your belt, you became both able and confident about performing on your own.

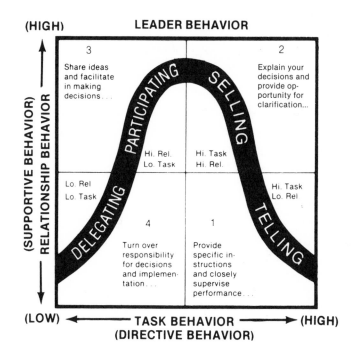

FOLLOWER CONFIDENCE

R4	R3	R2	R1
Confident	Insecure	Confident	Insecure
FOLLOWER DIRECTED		LEADER DIRECTED	

Illustration 5

It is important with Situational Leadership to recognize that there is nothing negative or wrong with being at any level of readiness for a particular task or function. Readiness describes the degree of ability and willingness a follower brings to a specific job.

Situational Leadership is just "organized common sense." An understanding of the model allows you to make better sense of the world around you and to understand why some behaviors haven't always worked for you. You'll recognize *why:*

* first line supervisors responsible for the development of new and inexperienced people find directing and closely supervising employees a useful leadership strategy, S1.

* enthusiastic followers who are eager to develop skills respond well to guidance and support, S2.

* employees that have the necessary knowledge and skill to complete a task but lack the confidence to take full responsibility respond well to encouragement and support, S3.

* executives who have experienced and committed followers can often get excellent results by letting them run with the ball, S4.

Being a Situational Leader works . . .

MATCHING STYLE AND READINESS

READINESS	STYLE	DESCRIPTOR
R1 Unable and unwilling or insecure	S1 HT/LR	Provide specific instructions and closely supervise performance
R2 Unable but willing or confident	S2 HT/HR	Explain decisions and provide opportunity for clarification
R3 Able but unwilling or insecure	S3 HR/LT	Share ideas and facilitate followers in decision making
R4 Able and willing or confident	S4 LR/LT	Turn over responsibility for decisions and implementation

Illustration 6

The illustration above combines follower readiness with leader behavior.

THE EPILOGUE

Rogers:

I guess what it boils down to is that in the different situations I have to face in managing people, I've got to be flexible in my behavior, and adapt to each situation in order to come across as consistent. The next step for me is to make sure I establish myself as the person in charge.

General Mgr:

Establish yourself as the person in charge?...What do you mean?...You're the boss; *aren't* you in charge?

CHAPTER FIVE

Taking Charge

THE STORY

Rogers:	I'm confident in my ability to pull this off. But, if there was one thing that Taylor emphasized to me as critical in moving into a leadership role, it was the importance of establishing a solid power base.
General Mgr:	What exactly do you mean by power?
Rogers:	Simply the things I have going for me as a manager that allow me to influence other people.
General Mgr:	Such as?
Rogers:	Well, the first thing that comes to mind is that they have to begin to view me as capable of providing rewards. And on the other hand, they certainly have to see me as not only able, but also as willing to impose sanctions.

General Mgr:	What's willingness got to do with it?
Rogers:	Most managers have the *ability* to carry out their responsibilities. Taylor was one of the few managers I ever worked for that was also willing to intervene in a problem situation.
General Mgr:	You know, I noticed that about Taylor myself. Why do you think it is that so many managers hide their heads in the sand when a problem comes up?
Rogers:	I think it's just that many people by their very nature don't want to be perceived as the "heavy." But, if there's a problem in the work place, and the person that's formally in charge doesn't do something about it, it can turn the whole group off.
General Mgr:	I've seen that one . . . and I like the idea of establishing control, but don't you want your people to like you?
Rogers:	Don't get me wrong. Getting people to like you, identify with

you, or see you as competent is important. But Taylor told me to remember that I don't control a friendship.

General Mgr: What do you mean, you "don't control a friendship?"

Rogers: Let's just take this interview as an example. I can walk out of here when we're done and think you're a tremendous person. I could *like* you an awful lot even after this brief period of time. But tomorrow morning, I could hear something about you or see you do something that would totally change my feelings of how much I liked you, and there's nothing you could do about that. But, no matter how much or how little I choose to like you as a person, you are still in control of the rewards and sanctions around here.

General Mgr: Hearing you say that makes me think of all the Management Development courses I've been to over the years that go out of their way to avoid the issue of power or control.

Rogers: Taylor used to comment on that ... but told me never to forget that power is a real world issue, and I'd better not try to sweep it under the carpet.

THE BACKGROUND

Influence Potential

When taking charge a leader must have the ability to influence. Leadership was defined as an attempt to influence another individual or group. In considering successful leadership the concept of power needs to be examined. *Power is influence potential.* Power is the resource that enables a leader to gain compliance or commitment from others.

Power is a subject that is often avoided. Power can have its seamy side, and many people want to wish it away and pretend it is not there. But, power is a real world issue. Leaders who understand and know how to use power are more effective than those who do not or will not. To successfully influence the behavior of others, the leader should understand the impact of power on the various leadership styles. In today's world many sources of power within organizations have been legislated, negotiated or policied away. Since leaders now have less power to draw from it is more important to be effective in the use of what is available. Since power bases drive your leadership styles, using them appropriately can enhance your effectiveness as a Situational Leader.

Position Power and Personal Power

Power can be divided into two basic classifications: Position Power and Personal Power.

Position power is defined as the extent to which leaders have rewards, punishments and sanctions they can bring to bear in reference to the followers. Position power comes from the organization . . . more importantly it comes from *above*. Position power can be thought of as the authority to use the rewards and sanctions that are delegated.

Keep in mind that just because you have position power today does not necessarily mean you will have it tomorrow. Not only can people above you delegate the authority to provide rewards and sanctions, but they can also take that authority away. This doesn't mean you cannot have an impact on how much you receive. The extent to which you develop confidence and trust between yourself and the people above you in the organization can determine how much authority they will be willing to delegate. Power is something you *earn* on a day to day basis.

Some important sources that contribute to a leader's position power are:

Coercive Power—based on fear. A leader who has coercive power is seen as inducing compliance because others perceive that failure to follow will lead to punishments such as reprimands, undesirable work assignments, or dismissals.

Connection Power—based on the followers' perceiving the leader to be connected to an influential or important person inside or outside the organization. A leader with connection power induces compliance because others want to gain the favors or avoid the sanctions that they associate with that person.

Legitimate Power—based on the followers' perceiving that it is appropriate for the leader to make the decision based on the leader's position or title. A leader who has legitimate power induces compliance because others feel that the leader has the right to decide by virtue of that position or title.

Reward Power—based on the followers' perception of the leader being a source of rewards. A leader with reward power gains compliance because others believe that following will lead to positive incentives such as pay, promotion, or recognition.

Personal power is defined as the extent to which you can gain the confidence and trust of those people that you're attempting to influence. It's the cohesiveness or commitment between leaders and followers. Personal power also has to do with the extent to which followers see their own goals as being the same as, similar to, or dependent upon the accomplishment of the leader's goals.

While position power comes from above in the organization, personal power comes from the willingness of the followers to follow. Personal power is not inherent in the leader. It has to be earned from the followers. Leaders do not have charisma. Followers give leaders charisma. This country reelected Richard Nixon with a landslide in 1972 and just a few months later, took back its commitment. Personal power is not within the leader, but comes from the people the leader is attempting to influence.

Some important sources that contribute to a leader's personal power are:

> Expert Power—based on the followers' perception of the leader's knowledge, skill, and expertise. A leader with expert power influences others only when followers perceive that expertise as necessary in satisfying their own goals and objectives.

> Information Power—based on the followers' perception that the leader possesses or has access to information that is valuable to them. A leader with information power gains influence because

of the followers' need for data or to be "in on things."

Referent Power—based on the followers' perception of the attractiveness of interacting with the leader. It's often the result of the leader being a good listener, acknowledging needs of others, and telling good stories. A leader with referent power is able to gain influence because others are willing to trade behaviors in order to continue the relationship.

A Best Power Base?

For nearly 500 years people have debated whether it's better for a leader to have position power or personal power. In the early 1500's Niccolo Machiavelli posed that question in his book, *The Prince.* Machiavelli was asking whether it's better for a leader to be feared or loved by the followers. His answer was that it's best for a leader to have *both* kinds of power.

Effective leaders do not rely exclusively on either power base. They build and sustain both. They do not shy away from the appropriate use of position power and, at the same time, continue to build their personal power.

Interactive Influence System

Even though position power and personal power are unique and distinct and have different sources, it is important to keep in mind that they form an interactive influence system. The two power bases directly affect each other.

When senior people see that a leader has the admiration and respect of the followers, they are more likely to provide that leader with additional authority and responsibility. At the same time, when followers see that their leader has the confidence of the people at higher levels in the organization and access to additional rewards and sanctions, they tend to give that leader more personal power. The extent to which followers are willing to follow depends a great deal upon their perception of the leader's ability to provide rewards, punishments and sanctions. Likewise, the extent to which the people above the leader in the organization are willing to delegate position power is often determined by the amount of personal power the leader has with their followers. Effective leaders earn personal power and build position power to maximize their influence potential.

A Matter of Perception

The key word in understanding power is "perception." It's not necessarily how much power leaders have, but how much power the followers *perceive* the leader is *willing and able* to use that evokes their behavior. Truth and reality evoke no behavior. All our behavior is evoked by our perceptions and interpretations of reality. How about the last time you had a fight with your spouse? It didn't matter whether the problem was real or imagined, it was just as big a fight.

Get the Data Out

With power, people must not only perceive you as having it, they must see you as able and willing to use it. Because power is a matter of perception, it is important that you get out the data. It's not enough to have access to power. You have to let people know you're willing to use it. You can't hide your light under a bushel. Information has no value in a data bank. It has value only when you get it out to the end user in a fashion that can be understood and accepted. It means simply, if you don't blow your own horn . . . . somebody else will use it as a spitoon!! Some leaders *have* plenty of power but are unwilling to *use* it.

Consider a father examining his son's report card and suffering mild cardiac tremors as he sees a solid column of "D" grades. Outraged that a product of his genes could so disgrace the family, he confronts his son and says, "Dave, this just won't do. I can't tolerate these grades, and if you don't show me an immediate turn-around, you're going to be grounded!''

Six weeks later Dave brings home another report card. This time the "D" grades are written in red ink with exclamation points. The father says, "David, get in here, I'm really upset, and now you have no choice at all. Hit those books hard, or you're definitely going to be grounded!''

Next time it's the same except that the teacher has added some pointed remarks about Dave's inattentive behavior in class. Dave's father turns crimson, crumples his beer can and shouts, "David Ralph, this is it . . . last chance city . . . you're in real trouble with the old man now!!''

What has Dave learned? That his father, who has the ability to ground him, won't use that power! Because of his Dad's reluctance to follow through with his threatened punishments, Dave knows that all he has to do is take heat for six minutes and he's "off the hook" for six weeks!

Power is a matter of perception—use it or lose it!

Power and Leadership Style

A Situational Leader needs to understand the relationship between power and application of leadership style. If a leader doesn't have a power base that drives a particular style, then even using that style appropriately may not produce desired results. Generally, when working with people at lower levels of readiness, position power will be the major influence source. For people at higher levels of readiness, personal power will tend to be the important influence source.

For example, if you are trying to gain compliance from someone who is unable and unwilling, you may have little success if you have no control over rewards and sanctions. Your "telling" intervention, no matter how appropriate, may be like water off a duck's back. Another example would be attempting to influence a follower where high relationship behavior might be appropriate. This behavior may be perceived as a punishment rather than a reward if you haven't built referent power. Building rapport is like making bank deposits. If referent power has not been developed, it won't be there to draw on when you need it. The Situational Leader develops and uses both position power and personal power.

THE EPILOGUE

Rogers:

The way I look at power, I not only have to establish my competence and continue to build rapport, but I also must be willing to pass out rewards appropriately and intervene in problem situations. If I can do that, I will be more effective in my efforts to accomplish the department's objectives and train and develop people.

General Mgr:

Train and develop people? . . . Aren't you going to have enough on your hands for awhile without trying to take over the training department's job too?

CHAPTER SIX

Growing Winners

THE STORY

Rogers:	I'm not trying to match the expertise that comes out of our training department, but I do think it's my responsibility to insure the development of skills of my people on a day-to-day basis.
General Mgr:	Let me guess . . . you and Taylor discussed a game plan for that too.
Rogers:	As a matter of fact, yes! I really don't mean to keep bringing up Taylor's name so much, but I can't remember respecting or learning as much from one person in my whole life.
General Mgr:	You were really committed to Taylor, weren't you?

Rogers:	You bet. Taylor said if you give your people the opportunity to stand on their own two feet and contribute, they will be motivated and grow.
General Mgr:	So how do you go about doing that?
Rogers:	The secret is in taking some risk and changing your style with people as their performance improves. If you maintain the same approach day in and day out, people have a tendency to level off and stay there.
General Mgr:	No risk, no growth, huh?
Rogers:	Exactly . . . the key seems to be cutting back on some of the guidance you provide a little at a time, observing performance, and then reinforcing improvement. That way you're taking risks, but they're calculated risks.
General Mgr:	Sounds a lot like the activity we go through at home trying to teach our kids the things they need to learn.

Rogers:	You're right...as a matter of fact, Taylor used to say the tragedy of the learning process is that it's often used only on the young.
General Mgr:	You're going to have to run that one by me again.
Rogers:	Well, let's take that job I had planning and preparing the budget. On the second "go around," Taylor was still there providing directions and watching my progress, but also provided opportunities to ask questions and get clarification.
General Mgr:	I see...having gone through it once you probably had some relevant questions to ask and a need to understand why you were doing it that way.
Rogers:	Right...and after I had done it well several times, Taylor felt I could do it on my own.
General Mgr:	How did that make you feel?
Rogers:	It felt great that Taylor had that kind of confidence in me, although I was still a little ap-

prehensive. As I remember, I got over that quickly because even though Taylor wasn't providing specific instructions, there was always the support and encouragement I needed. After gaining confidence, Taylor let me run with the ball on the budget. This autonomy and trust really made me feel like an important part of the team.

General Mgr: So that was that, huh?

Rogers: Almost. I don't want you to think that Taylor left me completely alone. We'd touch base on the budget now and then just to be sure I didn't head off in the wrong direction.

General Mgr: That's important too. So many times when managers delegate a project they think their job is done. Then they act surprised when they find out their people have taken the wrong offramp.

THE BACKGROUND

When assessing performance, both productivity and people need to be considered. Managers, teachers, and parents need to devote time to nurture their people's leadership potential, motivation, expertise, decision making and problem solving skills. The Situational Leader realizes the importance of developing their people. Human resources are critical for organizational success. In today's world the natural and technological resources are widely distributed. Recent literature concludes that human resources make the difference.

It is vital to emphasize the developmental responsibilities of the Situational Leader. Why? It can be summed up in the saying . . . . Give people a fish and they can eat for a day, teach people how to fish and they will eat for a lifetime. It isn't enough to simply provide the appropriate amounts of guidance and support for a given level of readiness. Situational Leaders develop the competence and commitment of their people so they're self-motivated rather than dependent on others for direction and guidance.

What's In It For the Manager

When followers are at low levels of readiness, the leader must take the responsibility for the "traditional" management functions such as planning, organizing, motivating, and controlling. The leader's role is that of supervisor of the group. However, when leaders develop their people and have followers at high levels of readiness, the followers can take over much of the responsibility for those day to day traditional management functions. The leader's role can then change from supervisor to the group's representative in the next level of the organization.

Through the development of people, Situational Leaders can invest their time in the "high payoff" management functions. These "linking pin" activities enhance the group's performance. When followers can take responsibility for their own tasks on a day to day basis, the leader can focus on these activities. These functions include acquiring resources necessary for maximizing the group's productivity, communicating both horizontally and vertically, and coordinating their group's efforts with other departments to improve overall productivity. The leader, instead of getting trapped in tunnel vision, has time for long range strategic planning and creativity.

Initially, close supervision and direction are helpful when working with individuals who have little experience in directing their own behavior. The Situational Leader recognizes that this style is only a first step. In order to maximize their potential in the high payoff functions, they must change their style and take an *active* role in helping others grow. The development of followers depends not only on the leader's behavior, but also on values and expectations.

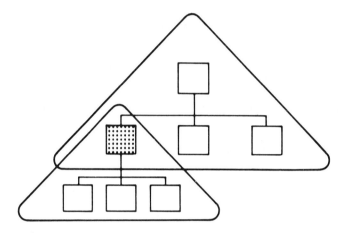

Illustration 7

The leader's role changes from that of supervisor of the group, to the group's representative in the next level of the organization. The leader then can perform the "high payoff" linking pin functions.

A Positive Belief in People

In working with people and helping them grow, managers need to have positive assumptions about the potential of others. Situational Leaders believe that people have the potential to grow and are confident that people can and will stand on their own two feet.

Followers' performance often mirrors the expectations their leaders have. Situational Leaders take responsibility for this potent impact they have on others. They recognize that if their expectations are high yet realistic, productivity and performance are likely to improve. When followers respond to the high expectations of their managers with high performance, the "effective cycle" has begun.

Leaders who do not see people as having potential and do not provide opportunities for growth, often reflect values that lead to lower performance. Low expectations of human potential can lend to low performance levels. Low performance then reinforces the manager's low expectations and an "ineffective cycle" may begin. The illustrations on the opposite page shows the effective and ineffective cycles.

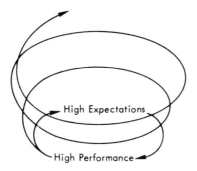

Illustration 8

The leader's high but realistic expectations lead to high performance of followers. The high performance then reinforces higher expectations and this leads to even higher performance.

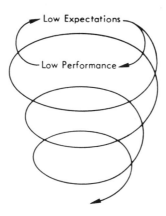

Illustration 9

The leader's low expectations may result in low performance of followers. The low performance then reinforces the lower expectations and produces even lower productivity.

It is important to remember that nothing stays the same. Things either get better or they get worse. The changes that occur with people can take place in spite of the leader or because of the leader. Situational Leaders are involved in and committed to planned change. Situational Leaders do not provide a crutch for the followers to lean on, but are catalysts for growth and development. They develop the readiness levels of their followers and take responsibility for making their people "winners."

Developing People

The first issue for leaders in developing people is: "What specific area of my follower's job do I want to influence?" Managers need to specify what good performance looks like. It is extremely difficult to develop followers' behavior in areas that are unclear. By identifying the *specific* outcomes, leaders can increase the accuracy of their diagnosis of the followers' readiness level.

The second issue for leaders is an assessment about the followers' willingness and ability for the identified activity. This will assist the leader in the development of the follower by using the appropriate leadership style.

Increasing Readiness

To explain how the Situational Leader develops people, let's consider an example. A manager determines that the readiness level of a follower is low, R1, for doing the budget. The manager begins the development process by directing the follower on what is involved and then showing the person how to do each part of the task. Although this "telling" style is high in direction and low in supportive behavior, this does not mean that the manager is not being personable or friendly. Low supportive behavior in this situation merely means that the manager is not providing more support than would be appropriate for the *current* performance.

In this case, the budget will be done fairly well since the manager is working closely with the follower. To increase readiness, the manager now cuts back, a little at a time, the amount of guidance provided. Thus, providing an opportunity for growth for the follower.

Take Calculated Risks

To develop followers, managers need to be willing to take some risks and delegate some responsibility. This is particularly true when supervising individuals who have not, in the past, assumed much responsibility. In taking risks to provide opportunity for growth, managers have to keep the degree of risk reasonable. For example, if parents want their own kids to learn how to do the dishes, what are they risking? The dishes. Therefore, it wouldn't be appropriate to start the kids out with Grandma's priceless bone china. That would be taking huge risks. It would be better to start them out with the melmac, the plastic. . . *a calculated risk.*

People Grow in Small Increments

Managers should remember that most people do not learn how to do things all at once. They learn a little bit at a time. Growth tends to occur in small increments. With this in mind, Situational Leaders take calculated risks when they reduce the amount of direction they provide followers. They don't set their people up for failure by telling them what to do and then leaving them on their own. The Situational Leader engages in a two step process that facilitates the followers' growth and development.

When developing followers at lower levels of readiness, the first step is to reduce somewhat the amount of direction and supervision. The leader then observes the follower. If desired performance follows, the second step would be to increase the amount of relationship behavior. Illustration 10 shows this process.

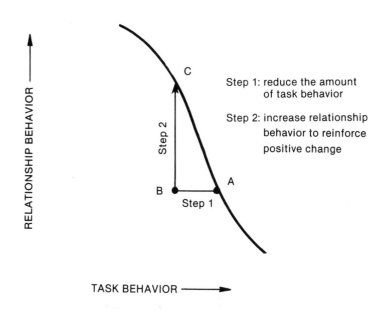

Illustration 10

To develop people, the manager delegates some responsibility by decreasing task behavior to point B (Step 1). If the follower responds well to the increased responsibility, the manager positively reinforces this behavior by increasing relationship behavior to point C (Step 2).

It is important to remember that a leader must take calculated risks and be careful not to delegate too much responsibility too rapidly. If done before the follower can handle it, the leader may be setting the follower up for failure and frustration. Thus, preventing that person from taking responsibility in the future.

Relationship Behavior as a Reward

Rewards and reinforcement are important tools for developing people. The use of supportive behavior is one of the few reward systems still available to managers. Therefore, it is important to use these rewards appropriately. Managers should provide rewards only when getting the desired performance.

While providing rewards, remember not to put the cart before the horse. If a leader cuts back on task behavior and increases relationship behavior at the same time, the follower would be receiving the reward before it was earned. It would be like paying twenty dollars an hour to a person who is worth only five dollars an hour at the time. If you give a person the twenty dollars up front, there may be little incentive left for improving their performance.

As People Grow, Their Needs Change

While people are at low readiness levels, they need structure and guidance from the leader. They also tend to view increased relationship behavior as a reward. The dialogue with the boss, the explanations, clarification, and pats on the back help to reinforce the change that's occurring as well as confidence and commitment.

As people grow to higher levels of readiness, their needs change. When they develop their ability to accomplish tasks, they no longer need as much direction and supervision. What they need then is support and encouragement. As people develop from moderate to high in readiness, less guidance and also less supportive behavior are appropriate.

This reduction of relationship behavior for people with high readiness does not mean there is less confidence and trust between leader and follower. In fact, it suggests there is more. Therefore, it is appropriate for the leader to reduce the amount of relationship behavior as followers at readiness levels 3 and 4 continue to grow. Situational Leaders, when working with people who are high in readiness, realize that what's occurring is that the need for autonomy is becoming stronger than the need for supportive behavior. Illustration 11 shows this process.

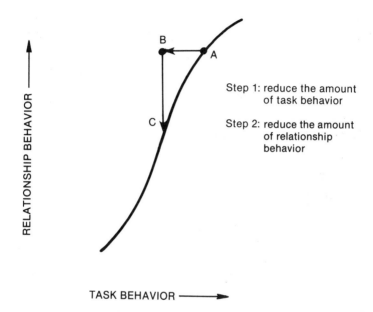

Step 1: reduce the amount
of task behavior

Step 2: reduce the amount
of relationship
behavior

Illustration 11

For people at readiness levels 3 and 4 the manager continues to delegate responsibility by decreasing the task behavior to point B (Step 1). If the follower responds well to the increased responsibility, the manager needs to provide less directive and supportive behavior because the follower is demonstrating their ability and confidence. (Step 2)

Use of Rewards

Situational Leaders realize that nothing in and of itself is a reward or punishment; it's in the mind of the beholder. What's rewarding for one person might be seen by someone else as punishing. It depends on a person's need satisfaction. Food for a hungry person will be looked upon as a reward. Food to a person who is full to the gills and is being forced to eat, may be looked upon as a punishment. It's important that the incentives a leader uses for improving performance are rewarding.

That's why it's appropriate to use increases of relationship behavior as rewards for followers at low readiness levels. If these followers were to be left on their own, it could be perceived as frightening. They may wonder where the boss is, if anyone cares about them, or what they are expected to do. In this case the leader's behavior could be seen as punishing rather than rewarding. However, with followers who are high in readiness, the opportunity to take responsibility and be on their own is often seen as a demonstration of trust and confidence and therefore rewarding. Situational Leaders attend to the needs of their followers and provide appropriate reinforcements.

When rewarding performance, the extent to which rewards are given should be directly proportional to the extent to which there has been change in the desired direction. Appropriate use of rewards by leaders is important. Parents, as well as managers, sometimes have a problem with this concept. They see a small behavior change in the desired direction and it's a, "LUV truck with a roll bar"; then there's nothing left for the teenager to aspire to. Situational Leaders provide small rewards for small amounts of change and significant rewards for significant change.

Should You Reward or Should You Punish?

Real problems can occur if a leader becomes over dependent upon punishment. This does not mean a leader shouldn't use punishment. It should be used with caution. When punishment is overused, a behavior may develop that's not directed toward goal accomplishment, but that's designed to avoid the punishment. For example, a child is "spanked" by a parent for not *looking* both ways before chasing a ball into the street. The next time the ball goes into the street the child may run to the street, *look* to see if the parent is anywhere in sight, then charge out into the street again to get the ball. So often behavior that results from punishment is designed only to avoid the punishment.

Start Development Early

When people are new to a job or project with little job related experiences, the time the leader invests in training and coaching can have a significant impact. However, people who have already established their own way of doing things may require more time and attention. They will have to unlearn inappropriate behaviors prior to learning or re-learning appropriate behaviors. More time and effort will be required to change established patterns.

Leadership situations can be looked upon either as a constant problem or an ongoing opportunity and challenge. The Situational Leader faces the challenges and seizes the opportunities to grow winners. The leader wins, the follower wins, and the organization wins.

THE EPILOGUE

Rogers:
The whole idea here is that some people will grow and develop almost in spite of what I do.... and then again many won't. The way I look at it, it's my responsibility to see to it that the people working for me have every possible opportunity to grow and contribute.

General Mgr:
This has been a real pleasure. It seems like you've covered all the bases pretty well.

Rogers:
Not quite.

CHAPTER SEVEN

Solving Performance Problems

THE STORY

General Mgr:	What do you mean, "not quite"?
Rogers:	I think it would be great if once I got people producing well and standing on their own two feet, they stayed that way.
General Mgr:	Certainly would make your job a lot easier, wouldn't it?
Rogers:	Yes it would. But I guess my concern is turning things around if for one reason or another people stop performing the way they did in the past.
General Mgr:	I have to be honest with you, coming down on people is not my favorite thing.
Rogers:	I doubt it will be mine either. . . but again, it's changing your style to match the level of performance that makes for effective interventions.

General Mgr:	Sure . . . just as you change while people are learning, you must also change if people start to slip.
Rogers:	Exactly . . . and not wait around hoping problems will just go away . . . they won't!
General Mgr:	Sometimes punishing people can be very uncomfortable.
Rogers:	Taylor preferred the term constructive discipline.
General Mgr:	What's the difference?
Rogers:	In constructive discipline, you attempt to correct performance in a timely manner without making the person angry or defensive. The goal is turning performance around, and providing people an opportunity for positive growth . . . not to slam dunk someone.
General Mgr:	Not an easy chore.
Rogers:	No, but if you catch things quickly and show specifically what the problem is, it certainly helps.

General Mgr: The problem I always seem to have is losing my temper.

Rogers: Taylor used to say that it is important to get people's attention when there is a problem, but screaming and yelling has a tendency to put them on the defensive and as a result, both parties wind up losing.

General Mgr: I've been there before.

Rogers: Me too . . . but I've learned that focusing on the specific performance issues can keep things in their proper perspective.

THE BACKGROUND

For one reason or another people's performance may begin to slip. One of the most difficult challenges leaders face is working with performance problems. That's because discipline is often viewed as a negative intervention. However, the origin of the word discipline is "disciple." A disciple is a learner.

Unfortunately in our culture many people interpret discipline as punishment. It is the problem solving nature of *constructive discipline* that differentiates it from punitive discipline. As such constructive discipline is designed to be a learning process that provides an opportunity for positive growth. Situational Leaders use constructive discipline when people slip in readiness.

A Look at Performance Slippage

Decreases in readiness occur for a variety of reasons. Followers can have problems with the boss, problems with co-workers, suffer burnout, boredom, and other problems on or off the job. These are just a few of the things that can have a negative impact on people's performance. Let's take an example of a performance problem.

An engineer was motivated and committed to the job and was excellent at the assigned task. It was not unusual to see the engineer in the office late at night and on the weekends. The engineer's boss was able to delegate and spend time engaging in the high payoff "linking pin" activities. However, things in the engineer's family life weren't going so well. The spouse saw the long hours and committment to work as a sign of not caring about their relationship. As a result, the spouse left. The engineer was shocked, and with the family problem becoming a major concern, effectiveness began to decrease. As the worries and concerns of the engineer increased, the performance on the job dropped. The delegating style the boss had used previously was no longer appropriate. The leader needed to go to a more facilitating or "participating" style so the performance problem could be worked on with the follower.

Situational Leaders recognize that when performance slips, they need to adapt their style accordingly. They don't ignore performance problems, but take responsibility for intervening and turning things around. Even when the delegating style is appropriate, they monitor results so they're aware if changes in performance occur.

Treat People Where They Are

When people's performance declines, the intervention needs to be made with a leadership style that is appropriate for their *present* readiness. Followers need to be *treated where they are* currently performing and not where they used to be. Not where their potential is.

Timeliness

Problem solving needs to be done in a timely manner. The sooner the intervention, the better the chance of stopping the performance slippage. The longer a leader waits, the more directive the intervention will have to be. Therefore, a leader may risk a follower becoming anxious, frustrated, or resentful. Even if the directive intervention is appropriate, this may lead to attempts to get out from under the leader or get the leader out.

For example, parents expect a child to keep their room clean. Over the past few months the child has done a good job at keeping it in good shape. Lately however, when the parents walk by the child's room, it's a mess. They begin to complain about the child's lack of performance to themselves, but still haven't talked with the child. Finally one day they have had it. The room is a disaster and they can't wait for the child to get home so that they can really let them have it. The child may then feel "zapped," be bitter toward the parents, and not focus on the importance of keeping the room clean.

If the parents had intervened earlier, a participative style would probably have been enough to turn the problem around. But now, the highly structured style is necessary and creates resentment in the child. This is a trap that leaders fall into when making disciplinary interventions. First they engage in "ostrich" leadership by sticking their heads in the sand and hoping the problem will go away. And then when it doesn't, they get angry and "zap" the follower. This all too common leadership pattern, S4 to S1, is called the "leave 'em alone, zap 'em" syndrome.

By timing interventions appropriately and treating people where they are currently performing, leaders can begin to take a proactive approach to problem solving as opposed to just reacting to each new crisis.

Varying the Emotional Level

The emotional level of the intervention is different for constructive discipline than it is for developing people. When developing people, you are attempting to expand the present ability of the follower. Therefore, it helps to keep the emotional content of a development intervention at a low level. People often misinterpret Situational Leadership because they think a "telling" style is raising your voice, hollering, or blowing your cool. Actually a Style 1 can be a very soft and caring approach by providing needed demonstration of how to do things with some "hands on" guidance. It would be inappropriate to shout at or raise the emotional level with people who are developing. It could tend to make them insecure about taking risks and continuing to learn in the future.

However, when followers choose not to use their present ability and constructive discipline is appropriate, you can raise the emotional content to a *moderate* level. This helps to get people's attention and lets them know that you are aware of the performance problem and that you care. It also helps to unfreeze the inappropriate behavior so that change can take place.

Focus on Performance

The next thing to consider in working with constructive discipline is; *don't attack personality,* focus on performance.

If you attack personality, and the person becomes angry, the probability of being able to successfully work with the person is much lower. So often a manager starts off a disciplinary intervention with, "I just told you that a week ago, can't you remember to do anything, you dumb son of a gun..." All this does is raise the emotional level of other people, but it doesn't get them to focus on the problem. If the focus is on performance, not personality, both leader and follower can talk about it and problem solve.

Be Specific. . . . Do Your Homework

Being specific about performance problems is important. When using constructive discipline, be careful of *glittering generalities.* So often managers on the job do all the other aspects of constructive discipline well; they treat people where they are, have good timing, keep a moderate emotional profile, and focus on performance. However, their intervention sounds like this, "Look, you're just not doing the kind of performance that we both know you're capable of; now let's get back on track." Then the manager is bewildered or gets angry when followers don't understand.

These kinds of glittering generalities don't get the job done. You have to do your homework before the intervention and gather specific details that may be useful in problem solving. With specific information the interventions might sound like, "Productivity is down $14\frac{1}{2}\%$," "Scrap loss is up $6\frac{1}{2}\%$," or "Project Z is 5 days late and we've got three other departments depending on us for that component." This provides specificity so that the leader and follower together can work on developing a solution.

Keep It Private

The last thing to remember is to keep disciplinary interventions private. As a guideline, it's a good idea to praise people in public and problem solve in private. If you address followers about problems when others are around, you run the risk of having them more concerned about being seen "catching hell" than on solving the problem. Discussing problems in private tends to make it easier to get your points across and keep the other person focused on the problem solving process.

The goal of constructive discipline is to make problem solving a positive, growth oriented opportunity instead of a punitive experience. It is important to:

* Treat people where they are presently performing
* Make the intervention timely
* Use an appropriate emotional level
* Focus on performance, not personality
* Be specific. . . . do your homework
* Keep the intervention private

Situational Leaders find that by keeping these factors in mind when making disciplinary interventions, discipline is not seen as a destructive intervention, but as a helping relationship.

THE EPILOGUE

Rogers:

I'm looking forward to this new position and I feel I'm prepared. As I look back on it, Taylor gave me an opportunity to be responsible for much of the department for the better part of the last six months. I know I can adapt my style to the various situations I will encounter. I'm excited about the opportunity, and after all, I think I had a pretty good role model.

General Mgr.:

This has been a worthwhile discussion and I'm looking forward to working with you. My intention this morning was to provide goals and objectives for your department, but as a result of our conversation. . . . let me "adjust my style." What do *you* think will be reasonable targets for the next quarter? . . . . .

CONCLUSION

AND WHO IS THE SITUATIONAL LEADER?

- A sales manager for a large insurance company.
- The night-shift supervisor for a coal mining company.
- An MBA managing a division for a major hi-tech firm.
- An elementary school teacher.
- A plant manager for an oil refinery.
- The parents of three kids.

It's anybody anywhere who recognizes that influencing behavior is not an event, but a process. The process entails assessing follower performance in relation to what the leader wants to accomplish and providing appropriate amounts of guidance and support. The Situational Leader is concerned about *people* and concerned about *results* and *behaves* in a manner where all parties win.

From cybernetics comes the law of requisite variety which suggests that in any system, all other things being equal, the individual with the widest range of appropriate responses will control the system. To achieve requisite variety as a Situational Leader you need two things: An awareness of the readiness of those you are attempting to influence and the ability to adapt your behavior to help others help themselves.

YOU CAN BE A SITUATIONAL LEADER...
...it's your choice!

POST EPILOGUE

General Mgr:	I've got to leave for a meeting in a couple minutes, but what do you say we get together late this afternoon. I'm really getting a lot out of this discussion.
Rogers:	I'd love to. But would it be possible to do it tomorrow instead? My husband and I are having dinner with Taylor and his wife, and I'm curious to hear about how his first day went.
General Mgr:	No problem, Suzanne. It's not critical that we talk right away...I have confidence in you and I know this department is in good hands.

In using Situational Leadership it is useful to keep in mind that there is no "one best way" to influence others. Rather, any Leader Behavior may be more or less effective depending on the Readiness of the person you are attempting to influence. The following model provides a quick reference to assist in, 1) Diagnosing the level of readiness, 2) Selecting high probability leadership styles and 3) Communicating styles to effectively influence behavior.

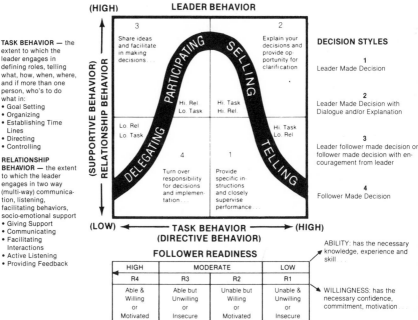

TASK BEHAVIOR — the extent to which the leader engages in defining roles, telling what, how, when, where, and if more than one person, who's to do what in:
- Goal Setting
- Organizing
- Establishing Time Lines
- Directing
- Controlling

RELATIONSHIP BEHAVIOR — the extent to which the leader engages in two way (multi-way) communication, listening, facilitating behaviors, socio-emotional support
- Giving Support
- Communicating
- Facilitating Interactions
- Active Listening
- Providing Feedback

(HIGH) **LEADER BEHAVIOR**

(SUPPORTIVE BEHAVIOR)
RELATIONSHIP BEHAVIOR

3
Share ideas and facilitate in making decisions...

PARTICIPATING

2
Explain your decisions and provide opportunity for clarification

SELLING

Hi. Rel.
Lo. Task

Hi. Task
Hi. Rel.

Lo. Rel.
Lo. Task

DELEGATING

Hi. Task
Lo. Rel.

TELLING

4
Turn over responsibility for decisions and implementation...

1
Provide specific instructions and closely supervise performance...

(LOW) ◄— **TASK BEHAVIOR** —► **(HIGH)**
(DIRECTIVE BEHAVIOR)

DECISION STYLES

1
Leader Made Decision

2
Leader Made Decision with Dialogue and/or Explanation

3
Leader follower made decision or follower made decision with encouragement from leader

4
Follower Made Decision

ABILITY: has the necessary knowledge, experience and skill...

WILLINGNESS: has the necessary confidence, commitment, motivation...

FOLLOWER READINESS

HIGH	MODERATE		LOW
R4	R3	R2	R1
Able & Willing or Motivated	Able but Unwilling or Insecure	Unable but Willing or Motivated	Unable & Unwilling or Insecure

Acknowledgements

Anything of quality is usually the result of more than one person. As such I would like to give recognition to the following people:

Ken Blanchard, a very special thanks for his contributions in the development of the Situational Leadership model and for his ongoing encouragement and friendship.

The names of the two Situational Leaders described in the story are not without significance. The names were inspired by two giants in this field, Frederick W. Taylor, the father of Scientific Management (Task Behavior) and Carl Rogers, who opened new horizons in interpersonal relations (Relationship Behavior).

Sandy Ogg, Sam Shriver, Kevin Sullivan, Tom Wunder for their contributions and assistance in the development of *The Situational Leader.*

Anna Donoghue, Jack Donoghue, Dewey Johnson, Bill Pfeiffer for their support and encouragement on this project.

About the Author

Dr. Paul Hersey is known internationally as an educator, trainer, lecturer, and conference leader. He has helped train over 1,000,000 managers and supervisors for more than 1000 business and industrial organizations. In the mid 1960's, Dr. Hersey founded the Center for Leadership Studies presently located in Escondido, California. His research at the Center led to the development of the Situational Leadership model. This approach to leadership in organizations has become a widely accepted managerial approach in the United States and other countries. Leadership Studies provides expertise and consulting in leadership, management, education, sales training, program development, and research.

INFORMATION ON HOW TO BECOME
A SITUATIONAL LEADER

For information on Situational Leadership and Situational Selling training programs, please contact:

Leadership Studies Productions
230 West Third Avenue
Escondido, CA 92025
(619) 741-6595

For information on instrumentation, publications, and related materials, contact:

University Associates
8517 Production Avenue
San Diego, CA 92121
(619) 578-5900